CW00448769

Introduction

One sat alone beside the highway begging,

His eyes were blind, the light he could not see;

He clutched his rags and shivered in the shadows,

Then Jesus came and bade his darkness flee.

When Jesus comes the tempter's pow'r is broken;

When Jesus comes the tears are wiped away.

He takes the gloom and fills the life with glory,

For all is changed when Jesus comes to stay.

Music by Homer Rodeheaver Words by Oswald J. Smith

As a child this song was on a tape that my gran used to play; I was probably around 4 years old and remember it while we played at her kitchen door. Many of the songs from that time are deeply embedded in my brain and pop up when I least expect them to.

One of the first times that I preached in church I had this topic as the theme of my message,

When Jesus comes;

I remember it so clearly, standing in front of a vast crowd of half a dozen people and revelling in the wonder of what this man Jesus could do. I was 19 and so hungry for God; He was everywhere, in everything that I did and thought; He was the answer to everyone's problems and I was full of love for Him.

22 years later, I am back to the same thought, but this time it's me that needs to hear it, it's me that needs to experience the touch of

Heaven as Christ comes into my life in all of His fullness once more.

Life has jaded much of that first love and I find myself in deep need to return to the sunshine and simplicity on the kitchen doorstep with my gran singing along as she worked at whatever it was grandmothers did in 1970's kitchens. The answer hasn't changed and never will as to what (or who) can fill and satisfy the great hole in the heart of a man; I want to go on this journey again and rediscover what I once knew, what thrilled me to my core at 19.

We can never, and should never seek to wipe out all of our experiences, good or bad, they make us who we are; but we need the touch of a higher hand to calm and soothe the pains of this harsh world.

I could save you a long read by answering the title of this book right here, the reason that I chose the title is because of the confusion that abounds regarding Christianity and church in general. What is it all actually about? Over the next eight chapters I want to explore the heart of God and His dealings with His ancient people; how He drew them, called them and worked with their failings.

Ultimately the answer to the title is simple, what does God actually want?

You.

1

As a race we come screaming into this world with the vanity and self-assurance that we are the centre of the universe. This thought is reaffirmed as we go through these first few years being photographed, pampered and generally having our every whim attended to. Of course it is correct and fitting that we are loved, cared for and protected in this way for that is the duty of care which is placed upon every parent. Would that every new-born arrived into such an environment, sadly many pregnancies are unwanted and babies lie neglected or malnourished in many countries.

We are seeing a rise in the cases of parents who fulfil the criteria of 1Timothy 3:3 who are "without natural affection." That said, it has turned very quickly to this point for various reasons, but I want to consider one of them.

In the late eighties when childcare moved from a parent directed responsibility to child centred and focussed (in the West) there was a societal shift in how we viewed ourselves. A generation before, our parents were finding a new freedom to express themselves in public demonstration and backed by popular music, they saw on their screens for the first time that there was more than just the parochial existence that their parents had lived. Which is strangely ironic, when you consider that so many men from that time were away for years fighting around the globe, and witnessing horrors that few ever again mentioned, especially to wives and children.

In America the post war boom gave way to civil unrest and an ever darkening society, the Communist spectre was raised and everyone became a possible enemy as the FBI under J Edgar Hoover raked through the intentions of all. The wars in Korea and Vietnam coupled with the Cuban missile crisis brought real fear and change to a proud and self-assured society. The assassination of the most popular of Presidents did nothing but unsettle the populace; it seemed to many that the cold war would run interminably. Tagged on to this was the civil rights movement that was changing everything in the lower states and sending shockwaves northward.

If you watch any movie from the 1980's it paints a very bleak picture of the city streets and an even darker dystopian future. It is true that the major cities were dangerous places to be, murder rates were high and crime was organised and rife.

Britain was not much better, the crippling 70's shortages had given way to an Authoritarian Government led by Margaret Thatcher who promised wealth for the few and taxation for the masses. She fulfilled her desire to return Britain to be a major player in the world again by rebuilding the economy; this came at the expense of the manufacturing and coal industries and the privatisation of many public sector organisations. The UK changed from a manufacturing centre to a service industry.

The yuppie culture on both sides of the Atlantic had erupted with great excess and enthusiasm putting vast sums of money into the hands of the lucky few. This lifestyle being reflected in TV programmes and the movie industry awakened a sleeping hunger in the hearts and minds of the general public; we all wanted a taste of that action.

For the first time a working man in Britain could own his own home and still afford to live; they wanted it all, the house, the car and the holidays and were prepared to do what took to get it; and so, many women hung up their aprons and set off out into the workplace to supplement the household incomes, gain freedom from domesticity and help pay for the expensive extras.

In the twenty five years since then we have experienced a monumental shift in public expectations; two wars in Iraq and one in Afghanistan have introduced us to a culture we had long overlooked; until 1990 most of the west viewed the middle East with a mixture of Lawrence of Arabian romance and as an oil rich sheikhdom with little impact upon our own lives.

It was the sudden impact of this culture on ours that showed in stark contrast how different the two cultures were; in one corner was the spoilt and increasingly self-absorbed safety of the West, and in the rest of the world everyone else with their dangerously uncivilised ways. That is, of course, a gross oversimplification of the larger picture, but I am concerned more with the overarching effects of the world situation than the cultural and historical intricacies for the purposes of this chapter.

Niall Ferguson in his 'Four Killer Apps of Civilisation" deals with this subject in a far more sweeping and comprehensive way (than I have the time or space to look at) which explores why the world shaped up as it did under the influence of a powerful island nation in the North Atlantic.

15 years ago a certain television executive dreamt up a new idea for a TV show and called it Pop Idol; it was to change the face of television worldwide and would make him immensely wealthy. It heralded in the instant celebrity and the desire awakened in every other teenager (and many who should have known better) the possibility of ultimate and instantaneous recognition. This was a tabloid dream, hapless teenagers and limited talent made for great newspaper sales. The show has

morphed into the X factor phenomenon and is syndicated worldwide with its attendant broken hopes and promise of instant wealth. Every year in many countries countless hopefuls pour into auditions looking for their own 15 minutes of fame. The reality phenomenon of Big Brother and many, many other people living lives in the TV glare has given rise to a selection of people famous only for their laxity of morals and dim wittedness.

Added into this melee we drop Facebook (1Billion users in a single day last week) closely followed by Twitter and then Instagram; we can all immediately upload our every whim and thought, live out our lives in public and get the instant gratification of recognition and 'likes'. What started out as a right to protest and express ourselves 50 years ago has snowballed into a maelstrom of self-absorption.

Had I been going chronologically through history I would have started in the garden of Eden, because that is where it (literally) all fell down for mankind. The promise of the serpent wasn't even subtle, although he is described as being so as he came to Eve saying, "you can be as God, knowing good and evil."

Ever since then, that is exactly what we have tried to do. Down through the ages of time men and women have sought to claw their way to the top of the pile at all costs and for however little a time, as long as they just make it there. The things that are today available to almost everyone were once the preserve of the ruling classes, as it was only they who had the wealth and freedom to indulge in such things (ice cream was found in stately homes for a 100 years before the 'penny Lick' made its way on to the streets of the cities with the influx of Italian immigrants into the UK. I should point out when I say 'everyone' that over 30% of the world's population don't have access to even the most basic of things that we take for granted in the 'so called ' developed world.

Unless you were being transported as a prisoner to Australia, or as a soldier or servant to America, foreign travel was nothing more than a pipe dream; it was the preserve of the aristocracy to go crashing through jungles or to go on the Grand Tour of Europe. Now, any gap year student can wander the globe and explore with the thousands of others going to the 'undiscovered' reaches of the planet.

The net result of all of this in Britain is that the average teenager from a middle income family has every electronic gadget available, they have the best clothes and shoes, and they will probably go to University and have been at least one foreign holiday. They live in a privately owned house and if they have a school prom will go to it in a £200 dress inside a stretch limousine.

 For them, being a celebrity is a viable career path.

When we turn to church life it is little different. The majority of modern churches are the domain of the middle classes who fall into many of the same categories mentioned above; their kids are fully integrated and indoctrinated into this 'me' culture and will take a great deal of re-educating if they are ever to understand the true message of Jesus Christ.

With the advent of the celebrity everything (chefs, gardeners, hairdressers et al) the church has not been left unaffected; we have Christian stars and celebrity preachers who sign autographs as if it was the most normal thing in the world to be doing (it is the most normal thing in the *world*, but ought not to be in the church) we profess to follow a man who made Himself of no reputation who wrote His truth on the hearts of men and women and backed it up with power to overcome their sin and sinful lives, not signed in a book with a quill.

Jesus

We follow on in a history of men and women, who gave up their lives and careers to follow in the commission of the Holy Spirit, and like Moses,

"when he grew up, refused to be called the son of Pharaoh's daughter. He chose to share the oppression of God's people instead of enjoying the fleeting pleasures of sin. He thought it was better to suffer for the sake of Christ than to own the treasures of Egypt,"
Hebrews 11:24-26

The entitlement culture we have been reared in is contrary to all that the Bible teaches; that is not to say that we all give up our jobs and houses and go live in a monastery, or fly to a forgotten slum in Asia (although some are called to such service). We are called to live, work and raise families while also carrying on with the calling of God on our lives. He has the right to demand of us whatever He desires to, because, He bought us with His own blood, and as such we are not our own if we are truly His followers.

2

"As you grow up, always tell the truth, do no harm to others, and don't think you are the most important being on earth." -- Harper Lee

Wise words indeed, from the author of one of my all-time favourite books. To Kill a Mockingbird was a story that I studied at school for my English class; it was really the first book to grip my attention in a meaningful way. I loved everything about it because I could relate to so many of the characters; it doesn't matter where you live in the world there are basic human characteristics that manifest themselves over and over.

I haven't read the story again since I was 15 but it is etched so deeply into my mind that I can still imagine the stifling, still heat and the dusty streets that Scout ran along, pausing as she came to the edge of Boo Radley's house because of the perceived threat within. One of towns that we lived in for a time had a man very like Boo, he painted his little fisherman's cottage with tar, the wall, doors and roof were thick with it (I doubt that he ever had a leak but you could smell it from forty feet) so we all called him the tarry man. He was in his sixties and would cycle everywhere on an on old black bicycle. We would treat him in a similar way to how Boo Radley was regarded and often were chased from his door. It turned out that he was a very kind old lonely man, he was kind with his money and time and visited people on that old black bike; these details only surfaced after he was killed on the road, miles from home cycling off on another mission. He was simply a man who, having loved and lost, built a cocoon around his house as he sought protection from the cruel world. It is only with the benefit of hindsight and meeting many such people over the years that I now understand what was really going on.

We all hide ourselves and protect our hearts in different ways, his was just very visible.

I loved also the injustice that drove a principled lawyer to stand firm against a culture that was horrendously unjust towards its own citizens because of a pigmentation difference. It has been implanted into me that we help the underdog, give the voiceless a voice and as much as we are able, to stand up for those who can't stand up for themselves. That said, I was never a fighter nor ever wanted to be a soldier apart from in my own fertile imagination.

God calls, in every generation, certain people who are willing to stand, like Atticus Finch, against the sweeping tide of popular culture and the media driven mayhem that is generally accepted as normality. (The recent revelations about the character of this man in the sequel have done little to demur my abiding admiration for his previous actions).

Abraham was such a man. He lived in the metropolis of his day, rich in culture and wealth. He was a man of great importance and influence whom God put His hand on; what was it that God saw in Abraham that he was chosen from among his peers?

It is a popular myth propounded today by many that we can all be something great and go on to achieve whatever we can dream (sorry Mr Disney, we don't all have you're resources).

The story of the Bible is one of ordinary men and women who went reluctantly into the work of God fearing for their very lives and future. There are always exceptions to this, King David being one, but the majority were called in spite of themselves. That is not to say that we must be timorous or backward in the work of God, apologising for living and doing what we are called to do. When God does empower someone they are usually an anomaly to most who previously knew them; filled with a boldness and the assurance that only God could give them, they step out from the crowd and confront kings saying 'is there not a cause?'

Abraham's dad had left the city of Ur and had taken with him everyone mentioned in chapter 12 of Genesis; it in interesting that he was headed for the very place that his son was to go to and would receive as an inheritance some 600 or so years later. There is no mention of a return journey from Haran but it must have taken place for in chapter 12 God calls Abraham from Ur (in modern day Iraq, probably the precursor to the site recently destroyed by ISIS). He is told to leave the place, his country, his relatives and his father's family. It is only an assumption, but perhaps he returned to bury his father and just stayed on. The call on his life is recorded in the past tense, "had called" so was it reiterated a second time? We will never know for sure, but what we do know is that he packed up and left as the head of the household.

Abraham had in him a strength of character that he wasn't aware of at the time of his call, he had enough gumption to uproot his entire family and all of their livestock and servants; but it would take many years for him to receive the promises he had been given. Many people in our day and down through the ages of time have cried out to God and been given a multiplicity of promises. When this happens, we all tend to react in the same way; we think that somewhere between now and two weeks from now God will make good on His promise. In my own experience that is seldom the case, study the history of God's dealings with mankind and you will find out that it was seldom the case with anyone. We imagine that because He has revealed something to us that we must be ready at that exact moment to receive it. More often than not the promise or vision is just the first step on a very long journey we must take. Abraham's journey took all of his life, he received the seed of the fulfilment and the joy of a son, eventually, but most of his promises remained still future at his death. We are going to look at how God called a nation in the next chapter, but I wanted to lay the bedrock about how this great nation came to be. Without a faithful Abraham, there was no Israel.

Of all the things said about Abraham in the word of God there are (for me) three things that stand out as defining characteristics. We asked what it was that God saw in him that he was to be the man on which to build a nation?

The first answer is found in the book of Romans, where in chapter 4 it is recorded that

"Abraham believed God, and it was counted to him for righteousness."

Secondly this nation was to be one that was built on righteousness and justice (Isaiah 54:14).

Thirdly the scriptures refer to Abraham as the **'friend of God'** which we will consider. These were the traits that I believe God saw in this man that he could work with.

So firstly let's look at his simple faith. We are told in Hebrews 11:6 that,

"Without faith it is impossible to please God"

In Romans 4, Hebrews 11, and James 3 we have a clear account of the faith of this man. He was someone who believed God! Not like these modern preachers who tell us we can have whatever our hearts desire if we can muster up enough faith; no, he simply believed what he was told. God said go, he went, and it was that basic. When we read the New Testament passages we would be forgiven for thinking that he was some kind of super-saint; a lot of his doubts and wrangling are never mentioned. I have long wondered why the Holy Spirit recorded it in this way when we are plainly told of his years of trying to work the whole thing out on his own while he lived through it. I believe the answer is simply one of grace; the overall tenor of Abraham's life was that he ploughed on in faith, **"when there was no reason to hope, he had hope"** Hebrews 11.

What we must always remember when reading the Bible is that we can read everything about this great man in less than an hour, but he lived for 175 years. I love that although we will give an account of our lives at the judgement seat, the overwhelming grace of God has already covered the mistakes by the blood of Jesus Christ. He looks at our hearts desires, we will always fall short of His perfect will for us, we may even behave like petulant children and storm off into foolish living; but like this great man, who made grave errors on several occasions, we are so profoundly loved by God That He is able to overlook our weaknesses and failures.

The first step we must make is one of simple direct obedience; whether you believe that God only communicates today through His word, or believe He can also speak directly to us the answer is the same. Do not get bogged down with the 'big names' on either side of that argument.

Don't complicate what God has made simple, if you ask for something and have an overwhelming conviction about it, then act! You will never move forward if you do not act on the things that you see from Scripture, it's a very basic principle that obedience to what you now know is the key to learning more.

First leave Ur!

If you were going to start a new country, what would be the first building block in your mind, take a minute to think about it.

On the 17th September 1787 a group of men sat down in a room to do exactly that, this is the first paragraph of what they wrote:

We the People of the United States, in Order to form a more perfect Union, establish Justice, insure domestic Tranquillity, provide for the common defence, promote the general Welfare, and secure the Blessings of Liberty to ourselves and our Posterity, do ordain and establish this Constitution for the United States of America.

Justice, it seems, was foremost in their minds; they reacted against the many injustices of the British imperial rule and stoutly decided to do it very differently. When God picked Abraham, it was righteousness and justice that were to be the foremost characteristics of this new nation. It was to take around 600 years before they had a land to call home and the same amount of time to get the, as yet, unborn people to exist. They would be formed in the slave pits of the most enduring ancient Civilisation, their strength of character and determination are as legendary as their suffering since that day to this. They are as clever as they are despised, but their father is Abraham and he is the first stone in their grand edifice.

When he was called, he knew none of this; he was unaware of what treasures were buried in his heart, the journey to Canaan was to be the making of him in many ways.

When Lot was carried away captive Abraham's protective instinct gathered his 318 men together to set off and rescue him; it was a rebellion he had no part in, but he weighed in because it affected his own family. He did something a general should never do and divided his men, but they were trained well and because they trusted him implicitly they were ultimately victorious. This was a man of great principles and trust in the provision of God; a lesser principled man would have gladly taken his share of the spoils of war (read the story in Genesis 14).

It is often the case as we step out in obedience that the further along the road we go with God we are forbidden from doing as the world would. Things that are a right and not necessarily evil are increasingly out-with our range of acceptability; things that even Christians take for granted become unavailable to those who chose to walk closer. It sounds like a two tier Christianity but it is simply that walking close to Lord disallows practices and thought processes that many don't even think twice about. Is it that He doesn't want others to enjoy this fellowship? No, it is more that we decide to settle for a greatly reduced walk, much less than He would have us enjoy. We will look at how a nation made this decision in chapter three but many over the years have done the same; Demas for one, chose to go home rather than enduring the rigours of a life with the Apostle and the constant rejection that came with him (2 Timothy 4:10). I have great sympathy for Demas, what little we know about him is negative but the hardness of the Christian road can wear a person to powder at times; maybe he just needed a break to regroup and build up his resources again.

The next time Abraham had this sense of injustice aroused was also in relation to Sodom and affected Lot. The Lord in His pre-incarnate form comes to Abraham's tent door and shares a meal with him (Genesis 17 & 18). He tells the great man again about the birth of his son before the passing of a year; this is the first time that he has a specific timescale put on the fulfilment of his promise. As the trio are walking away they pause and tell Abraham the purpose of the visit is also to destroy Sodom and Gomorrah, the twin towns of wickedness in the valley below. The rest of us would probably have looked at the situation and rationalised that it was totally justified to clear them from the earth; but deep in the heart of Abraham something stirred.

What then followed was a man pleading the character of God with Him; I don't believe that God changed His mind as much as He put this situation in front of Abraham in order to reveal the purpose of his life and the character that was essential to the foundation of it.

In a town in 1960's Alabama a man was stirred to stand up and lead a cultural revolution, he was eloquent and charismatic and it cost him his life; but consider what would have happened (or not) had he said no when the leaders of the civil rights movement asked Martin Luther king to be their rallying voice.. As with so many others who have found themselves in pivotal moments of history it was seemingly small initial decisions that led to great change coming about. We all face these decisions, whether it be to declare our faith at work, or to remain devoted to our partners and raise our children with integrity in an increasingly morally corrupted world.

The third thing we want to consider is that Abraham was called a friend of God. Bear in mind that there were no churches, no temples, and no tabernacle in which to meet with this God who was communicating with him. He was out there on his own with a wife and nephew and many other people tagging along, looking to him for answers and direction; they had stepped out with him on his calling. Of course, the nomadic lifestyle was not at all unusual at that time but it had not been *their* life up until now.

Like all friendships, his began with a step in a mutual direction. Everyone that you or I have ever had a friendship with began at the point where we both converged on the path of life; some are privileged to have lifelong friends, that has not been my experience.

As a child we moved around a fair bit and as such I had (of necessity) to become good at making new friends. The secret to this is being open; some people are in your life for a very short period of time and you can miss all that they are and have to share with you if you are guarded with your emotional availability. The dangerous part of living like this is that we open ourselves up to all manner of hurts; I would say that it is well worth the risk. The richness that friends can bring, the sudden closeness of a person from the other side of the world enhances and enlivens the Christian experience immensely; I have met the most amazing people over the years simply by being open to engage with strangers in church or elsewhere. People whom I often wonder what became of them who walked with me for a couple of weeks or months and then vanished as their lives marched on in new directions. This is not an easy way to live; some people find the transience of it too difficult to cope with, but the fleeting time we get with each of the friends makes the walk that bit fuller.

Abraham started out on this journey with God at the point of his obedience; I believe that God is looking in every generation for those willing to go that bit further than mere obedience. Such is His capacity that this number can be any size and yet still experience the fullness of His presence and as much of His attention as we are able to bear. What Abraham experienced was recorded for us, but only the scarcest details of his long life are there, in between there was the daily fellowship that he must have enjoyed with all of its frustration and wondering. These men were just like us, remember, and they thought the same thoughts and had the same questions. What was it that got him to the point where the Lord couldn't hide from him that He was about to destroy Sodom? Like every friendship it took years of mutual respect and love, trust and talking together; this was not a fast immediate friendship, it was a slow burning, trust building, getting to know each other intimately kind of friendship. Such was the mutuality that the Lord included Abraham in such large decisions; as we have pointed out it was also for Abraham's benefit in drawing from him something that he never knew was there.

When God asked him to sacrifice his long promised son, he didn't hesitate; he reasoned that whatever happened this child was God's plan 'a' and there was no plan 'b'. So even if the child was to die then he would be raised again to life; there was no precedent for this happening but such was his trust that he had

"hope when there was no reason to hope."

Abraham sits in his place in history as one of the few men of whom it was said 'friend', Moses also ranked among the few and Noah, Enoch and Elijah walked closely with their God in their own generations. Such a privileged opportunity is open to each of us if we will choose it; to rise above the norm and go deeper, further and closer than the many dare to.

3

We have seen how it is possible for a man alone to walk with God, to scale the heights of the unknowable and receive there a measure of revelation open only to the earnest seeking heart. Abraham was to become the father of all the faithful, but initially he was to be the father of a nation.

The beginnings of this nation were humble to say the least, a wandering Chaldean with a call from the Almighty God heading out into the unknown with a promise of more.

God had clearly told Abraham that his family would become great and would go down to

Egypt where they would remain for 400 years, becoming slaves in the process (Genesis 15). It would be his great grandchildren that would be the generation to go there because of famine. Abraham was blessed by God to see his twin grandsons grow to be teenagers, although the record isn't clear, a simple arithmetic calculation tells us:

he was 175 when he died

he was 100 when Isaac was born

Isaac was 60 when Jacob and Esau were born

So often in the Old Testament we find that the lives of the great characters overlapped and a little scraping of the surface reveals by how much. We are in danger of forgetting that they had strong family ties and were not a series of random, standalone men and women standing in historical line.

The story of Joseph is embedded in most minds thanks to the Andrew Lloyd Webber musical, but this man was something of a fighter. He had a barrel load of character and seemed undaunted and undefeatable; in truth he truly was. God was working behind the scenes giving him favour in one difficult situation after another to ensure that he was exactly where history required him to be at the exact moment he needed to be there. So many of us living through horrendously unjust and difficult circumstances have as little overall perspective as Joseph did. He wasn't rejoicing in his misfortune at the time, it was only by the time that his brothers came pleading for food that he had gained perspective on his life. We must never be too hard on ourselves when everything is going wrong, it is possible to get perspective in the circumstances but often it isn't until much later that we can see it with any measure of clarity. I should add that sometimes we never get to understand what it was all about, that will need to wait until we reach the other side.

There was always something about the brushing of Joseph from the Egyptian records that bothered me. Here was a nation that was known for its accuracy in recording even the most infinitesimal details of daily life and yet a Pharaoh rises to power who knows nothing of Joseph and his pivotal role in their history. Granted, several hundred years had passed and a long distant famine may not have registered high on the radar of a man who saw himself as a deity. Even the presence of a million or more non indigenous people may have done little to pique the curiosity of a self-absorbed, pompous king hell bent on establishing his own grand legacy; perhaps not such a stretch after all. Because we skip so gently over the three centuries with the Joseph story so fresh in our minds, we find it incredulous that such a long time has passed. Could many of us name the vice president or deputy prime minister from even 100 years ago without Google.

Over these many years this 'chosen' people had lived and died, grown in numbers and been subjugated as God had predicted so long before when speaking to Abraham; their existence had degenerated to the most servile of places and they were crying out to God for deliverance. It is comforting to know that their cries were being heard and God was again preparing a man who was to be their great leader. I am sure at the time when Moses was born that the people would have welcomed freedom, but in the divine purposes eighty more years were to pass as Moses was schooled in the culture of Egypt and then the school of God in the wilderness.

How often have I tried to rush the Lord, only this week I was saying to My wife that I wish I had known ten years ago what I was being prepared for. The frantic pace of the last eight years and all that we were involved in seems like a blur in some ways; however, the blessing of being used in the service of the Lord are huge even if the price He demands is equally great.

Be careful what you say to God, I clearly remember saying that I was willing to be used in any way that it took to accomplish what He desired in our town. The reality of that was extremely hard at times and, while very rewarding, being 'used' is often until empty, wrung out and dry. Please don't think that He will only use us as we see fit!

When Moses was sent to Pharaoh he had a very specific message from God,

"The LORD, the God of the Hebrews, has met with us. So please let us take a three-day journey into the wilderness to offer sacrifices to the LORD, our God." Exodus 3.

They could not begin in this new relationship that God was calling them to while still under the staff of oppression; it was essential that they had distance from that regime and could settle in a peaceful place to fully focus on what God was saying to them. When we are called to follow Christ, no matter what has been our background, we will usually need to put a distance between what we were and what we are being called into. The influx of the Holy Spirit which we receive at salvation puts fire in our bones and fills us with such a desire after God and His things that to stay where we were is a near impossibility. Naturally all of us experience this to a greater or lesser extent, but if there is no change of desire awakened within us at all we must surely ask if we were truly reborn; for by very definition something new has begun inside of us and the new life which the Holy Spirit brings is a revolutionary transformation in a sin dead soul.

That which was in the heart of God in calling an entire nation was the same desire that had been expressed as He spent those times in the garden with Adam and Eve. His heart has never changed, fellowship is His great desire, it was what spurred Him to begin this great creation and knowing what it would ultimately cost Him, continue on to pursue a people for Himself.

After bringing this vast multitude out from their slavery by the ten plagues which culminated in the angel of death and the redemption by blood; this mobile nation decimated Egypt as they left, walking as free men and women for the first time in living memory. Of course, the anger of Pharaoh rose quickly as his remorse flamed into action; he pursued them into a corner where once again he witnessed the power of a God whom he refused to acknowledge. It would be the last thing that he would ever see.

The lessons we can learn from a wandering nation for our own lives could fill a library of books, my interest, however, is primarily in the intention of the heart of God in calling them to Himself in such a unique way. When we catch up with them at the foot of Sinai, two months after leaving Egypt, we hear what this calling is to involve, it is so much more than just a three day journey to worship Him;

'You have seen what I did to the Egyptians. You know how I carried you on eagles' wings and brought you to myself. Now if you will obey me and keep my covenant, you will be my own special treasure from among all the peoples on earth; for all the earth belongs to me. And you will be my kingdom of priests, my holy nation. 'This is the message you must give to the people of Israel." Exodus 19.

This was something completely different and new, nothing like it had ever been known and has never since then been done again. This audacious plan could only have originated in God, no mere man could have dreamt this up and brought it as a proposal to the divine; an entire nation of priests. Not a select few in an intermediary position performing the role of spiritual leadership on behalf of the masses. How different would the following chapters have looked had they said yes? We could postulate and speculate many variables of the outcome, but ultimately we must return to the sad reality of what the people replied in the face of a Holy and Awesome God. Initially it was looking good...

And all the people responded together, "We will do everything the LORD has commanded. "So Moses brought the people's answer back to the LORD. Then the LORD said to Moses, "I will come to you in a thick cloud, Moses, so the people themselves can hear me when I speak with you. Then they will always trust you."

But

On the morning of the third day, thunder roared and lightning flashed, and a dense cloud came down on the mountain. There was a long, loud blast from a ram's horn, and all the people trembled. Moses led them out from the camp to meet with God, and they stood at the foot of the mountain. All of Mount Sinai was covered with smoke because the LORD had descended on it in the form of fire. The smoke billowed into the sky like smoke from a brick kiln, and the whole mountain shook violently. As the blast of the ram's horn grew louder and louder, Moses spoke, and God thundered his reply.

When the people heard the thunder and the loud blast of the ram's horn, and when they saw the flashes of lightning and the smoke billowing from the mountain, they stood at a distance, trembling with fear. And they said to Moses, "You speak to us, and we will listen. But don't let God speak directly to us, or we will die!""Don't be afraid, "Moses answered them, "for God has come in this way to test you, and so that your fear of him will keep you from sinning!" As the people stood in the distance, Moses approached the dark cloud where God was.

I may be mistaken, but I believe in that simple statement in verse 19

"You speak to us, and we will listen. But don't let God speak *directly* to us, or we will die!"(Italics added)

the people rejected the advances of God and His invitation to a personal relationship with Himself. The reassurances of Moses about the reason for the audible and visible display of His power did little to persuade them to retract what they had said. This God is way too scary, so when they ask Aaron later to fashion a god for them to worship it is a golden calf. Mute and approachable, safe and much more like the gods which they were used to back in Egypt.

Sadly, we do the same, in spite of looking askance from four millennia distant we each have opportunities in our Christian life to embrace the undiscovered God; When He pulls back the curtain to give us a glimpse of the fringes of all that He is, many are appalled and pull back like a little tortoise into their shell. We venture out when we think that it's safe to look again but are unable to bear the awfulness of who He is, so we fashion a version of Him that fits with our sensibilities and we are comfortable enough to cope with. We reconcile with ourselves that He is not culturally acceptable or that this God isn't relevant to our world and our refined ways; and you know what? We are totally correct, He never was acceptable, He never will be and He never should be. A God that we can rationalise and understand that we can fit into our world and feel comfortable with just isn't God enough to meet and satisfy the deepest longings in the hearts of men. So we make a word that can only truly be ascribed to deity be used to describe everything from a good sporting achievement to a tasty burger as we reduce 'awe' to the mundanity of the existence we can cope with.

So the nation that said no to the desire of God went on to treat the Promised Land with the same level of disdain, for how can we appreciate the Blessings of God if we don't understand the heart of God who is blessing? We can't value things the way He does if we don't see them through His eyes, the grapes are too small and the giants are too big; while in reality in the estimation of God the situation is reversed.

So a generation perishes a few days walk from their inheritance, and the Hebrew writer pleads with us to fear in case we would do the same. What a tragedy to live within sight of the blessing but never to experience it because of unbelief.

Of the two million or so people who left Egypt, no one over the age of eighteen was allowed to enter the Promised Land except from Caleb and Joshua, the two faithful scouts who spoke truth in the face of huge opposition. Even Moses was barred from entering because of the standard he failed to reach in being an example to the people, it seems harsh, but when we represent a Holy God we are required to work to His standards and no lower. I am required to check myself at times as I apply 21st century morals to a Holy God. Even as recently as the world wars people were executed for cowardice, the standard that they were expected to rise to was way lower than Gods and yet it was not considered wrong to shoot them for failing to meet it. And yet when we read of Moses being denied entrance to the land or Ananias and his wife being removed for lying we balk.

When the time finally came and everyone was ready to move forward into the land, an 80 year old Joshua strapped on his sword and led them in to victory over the resident population and a wandering nation finally had a land of their own.

4

Before we say goodbye to Moses and charge forward with the nation of Israel it would be good to explore a little bit deeper into the life of this man who (as much as Abraham) shaped the people during his lifetime. He was a man of great highs and desperate lows but he scaled heights in his relationship with God that few have equalled since.

His start in life was inauspicious, born at a time when it was illegal to be a Hebrew boy, his mother saw in him 'something' that she hadn't seen in his two elder siblings. Aaron and Miriam had slipped into this life unnoticed by the wider world and had grown up into children who knew nothing different from the hard labour of their parents lives. But this child was born in the midst of a great persecution where most of his generation were drowned at birth; we don't know how long that this policy of male genocide existed but there must have been a hole in the nation of men this age.

His mother was an astute woman, a Levite and in tune with the eternal purposes of God; as she made this little wicker boat she was determined to save the child alive if even for a few days at the mercy of the river. Desperation has a way of encouraging innovation and we could spiritualise her actions and say that she was guided by God in what she did (and in many ways she was) but she simply did what she knew how to do. In the grand scheme of things God was at work in the background arranging everything to ensure that this child was fit to be a leader eighty years in the future.

The Biblical principle is ever present as we see countless people give something up to preserve it, Christ Himself putting it into the plainest of language.

"If you try to hang on to your life, you will lose it. But if you give up your life for my sake, you will save it." Luke 9:24

So she gently pushed the little boat out on the water like the "casting of bread," the child that she had spent nine months carrying, then having gone through the agony of birth she nurtured and hid him for three tense months only to face the inevitable decision to send him out.

We in the West who are accustomed to high birth rates and unaccustomed to high infant mortality rates forget how much of a miracle each new-born is, with the knowledge that we now possess it should make us all the more to cherish each new life. Instead we are comfortable to allow a genocide of unborn children on a scale that puts previous generations actions in the shade.

It was too soon, he should be a carefree boy and in the course of time should develop into a strong young man; he should have enjoyed a dozen birthdays before this. What was the conversation with her husband that brought everything down to this as a viable option? How many have faced the same decision with the collapse of a vision and the end of a dream, packaging it up and sending it out on the river of time at the mercy of God. Some will receive it back as she does, but many watch as years of effort, sacrifice and labour float away downstream never to be seen again.

Unable to stay herself and watch the baby go, she leaves his elder sister to see what will become of him; the course of events that unfold could not have been written by the best Disney scriptwriter, what is the best case scenario you can hope for, not the unlikeliest, the best? The eye of princess herself falls on him as she bathes in the river, intrigued by the cries she orders the basket to be opened and in a turn of events that only the influence of God on her heart could have brought about, she has compassion on him. Miriam was no slouch either, she appraises the situation and dives in with a solution that pleases her highness greatly; we are not party to the particulars of what followed, but an arrangement was settled upon that gave payment for care and a return to the palace at an arranged date.

I have tried to put myself into the position of this couple at the close of such a day, many times we have ended a day wondering at the twists and turns of twenty four hours which settled into peace at the close. I can see them sitting shaking their heads as they gaze at this child, a few hours before he was all but lost to them and now he is there in their home under royal protection and they are carers by royal decree with an income as well. Nothing and no one can touch or interfere with a person who has a purpose; only under the decree of God himself can even Satan get near such a person.

Forty years are gone in a flash of privileged existence as Moses is schooled in the ways of one of the greatest civilisations known to man; he is given the best that life has to offer and an education that no other Hebrew was ever to experience since the days of Joseph. There is no indication of any contact with his family, however, there is equally nothing to say that they didn't have regular contact; he was obviously aware of them and knew of his brother Aaron, as God had sent him to meet Moses on his return journey (Exodus 4).

It is always interesting to see the beginnings of a man's passion when it surfaces in spite of himself, many men have stood where Moses did at forty and surveyed the aftermath of something that they never knew was in them until after the event. Thankfully we don't all go killing someone in order to reveal our passions, but the principle is the same as Abraham looking over Sodom, or a David listening to a defiant Goliath. Down through the ages men and women have risen to the challenge of injustice and stepped out of their own comfortable lives for the sake of others; for Moses, it was a position of exaltation that he left, to hide in the wilderness far from all that he had known.

The Hebrew writer fills in the blank...

"It was by faith that Moses, when he grew up, refused to be called the son of Pharaoh's daughter. He chose to share the oppression of God's people instead of enjoying the fleeting pleasures of sin. He thought it was better to suffer for the sake of Christ than to own the treasures of Egypt, for he was looking ahead to his great reward."

(Hebrews 11:25-27)

I think it would be easy to question the motivation of a person like myself who never really had much in a worldly sense to give up; I have, but while wrestling with it recently I realised that you don't necessarily need to have something in order to give it up. True, many people have relinquished positions of influence and wealth or addiction and squalor; to leave these places requires an equal amount of will power and Holy Spirit power, however if (like me) your life wasn't one of great excess we can be fooled into believing that we are somehow disqualified from radical obedience and making these choices. I have come to realise that it was God's protection over me that preserved me from excess in my teenage years and from dangerous situations that would have made it very difficult to do what He has since led me into.

We can choose to relinquish what everyone in our generation is chasing, we can choose to live by a different standard and to the beat of heaven's drum instead of that of the world; we don't need to have been rich, powerful, addicted or cast out in order to be a prodigal we are all tarred with that same brush by nature.

I have long since learned that With God timing is everything, He will take however long it takes to prepare a man, or a nation or a bride to be ready for the specific purposes that He has in mind.

Forty years of pampering and training gave way to forty years of shepherding and family life in seclusion for Moses. The grandeur of Egypt was replaced with the comfort of a tent and an extended family unit; days gave way to years spent with a flock of sheep in the hills as Egypt's arrogant edge was mellowed out of the Man who would become among the meekest of all men.

The gentle shepherd life couldn't have been more different to his previous experience, suddenly he was loved and accepted by this close family, each night would be a shared meal around a fire after a long quiet day with the animals. Family became his everything, that's all that there was out there, instead of being pampered, bowed to and revered, he was becoming peaceful, level and loved.

Perhaps he would have happily lived out his days like this, content to be a father and shepherd unknown outside of this narrow confine; God had other ideas, this was stage two of his training and one day the call of God fell on his eighty year old ears.

His day began like any other and ended with him as a murderer and a fugitive forty years previously, and on another day like every other he saw something that would change every day from that one forward. Deep in the heart of the wilderness a bush was burning without being consumed, a bush on fire wasn't all that unusual to him but on fire and not being consumed demanded a closer inspection. There are no limits to the imagination of our God, he will use whatever it takes to get our attention, He knows the very thing that will pique our curiosity to start us on the road to his heart. First and foremost in all of this book and this chapter is the truth that He wants **me**, He wants my heart and my love and my time and my attention; the very thing that the nation said no to in the last chapter Moses had said yes to on this first morning by the bush. His journey with God began in earnest right here, up to this point in his life it was all background guidance, now it was time for the lifetime of personal communication with a Holy God. It matters nothing at what age we begin, it matters only that we do begin and how far we then go is completely dependent on how far we want to go.

When God introduced Himself to Moses in Exodus chapter three He called Himself

"The God of your father - of Abraham, Isaac and Jacob."

 Whatever the link Moses had with his dad had been sufficient for him to understand who this God was and caused him to avert his gaze from the bush; he understood that he wasn't talking with some Egyptian king who claimed to be God but with the God of his ancestors. This initial meeting established in Moses' mind forever the nature of the God he was dealing with, he never lost sight of this experience and in all of the highs and lows of their subsequent relationship over the next forty years he only built on what he had begun that day.

"The sail was patched with flour sacks and, furled; it looked like the flag of permanent defeat."

This is taken from the first chapter of Ernest Hemmingway's classic, 'The old man and the sea' and it sums up the experience of so many mature Christians as he describes the skiff sitting by the harbour wall after numberless unsuccessful fishing trips. Moses was coming to the end of a quiet forty years, he was eighty years old and in the minds of many should have been looking to see out his final years in a peaceful retirement. I have read so many books and listened to as many testimonies that edit out the barren periods where we sit like a clipper in the doldrums, deafened by the silence and still on a glassy sea. My own experience is one of sublime highs and desperate lows, I can relate to the old skiff today; I can write from knowing the deep experience of the **"fullness of joy"** but it is a memory just now rather than and current reality. I always wanted to be brutally honest in writing this and it is a journalistic voyage that I pray will end in the Father's heart once more.

From day one at the bush, Moses had an open hearted relationship with God, he felt free to debate and question the task in relation to himself and his abilities; his reverence was never in question but his flat out obedience was. He bargains with God and goes to Egypt in a lesser capacity than was his original calling; some have taken this to be licence to question and argue with God about His direction but we must defer to the perfect servant for ultimate guidance in these matters. Christ Himself who,

"Did only those things that pleased the Father"

All other men are just that, men.

It was never my purpose to exhaustively analyse the life of Moses, simply to see his interaction with deity and perhaps learn a little from him. On his many trips up the mountain and into the tent of meeting to be with God throughout the Pentateuch it is apparent that in Moses, God found something that he liked, we are told that,

"Inside the Tent of Meeting, the LORD would speak to Moses face to face, as one speaks to a friend. Afterward Moses would return to the camp," (Exodus 33:11)

As the leader of well over a million people, he needed this refreshing from God's presence or he would never have been able to continue, he had no government or even structure in place until his father in law suggested a plan (let's hear it for Godly father in laws). His primary function was to lead them out of Egypt to meet with God and then lead them into the land as a kingdom of priests; what actually transpired was not the intention of God, but the result of a rejection by the people of God's advances.

In God's mercy Moses walked daily in His presence and relayed that presence by default to everyone else in the camp as they saw the Glory of God on his face (albeit covered because even that was too much for them to bear). This daily interaction led one day to a request from Moses for more; he wanted everything that it was possible for a mortal man to have while on earth.

Exodus 33:13-23

If it is true that you look favourably on me, let me know your ways so I may understand you more fully and continue to enjoy your favour. And remember that this nation is your very own people." The LORD replied, "I will personally go with you, Moses, and I will give you rest—everything will be fine for you." Then Moses said, "If you don't personally go with us, don't make us leave this place. How will anyone know that you look favourably on me—on me and on your people—if you don't go with us? For your presence among us sets your people and me apart from all other people on the earth." The LORD replied to Moses, "I will indeed do what you have asked, for I look favourably on you, and I know you by name." Moses responded, "Then show me your glorious presence." The LORD replied, "I will make all my goodness pass before you, and I will call out my name, Yahweh,* before you. For I will show mercy to anyone I choose, and I will show compassion to anyone I choose. But you may not look directly at my face, for no one may see me and live." The LORD continued, "Look, stand near me on this rock. As my glorious presence passes by, I will hide you in the crevice of the rock and cover you with my hand until I have passed by. Then I will remove my hand and let you see me from behind. But my face will not be seen." (NLT)

For most of us, even to experience what Moses did on a daily basis would be phenomenal, but to then ask for this? The audacity of his thinking about what was available to him was in itself tremendous, but to get the response that he did was amazing. Now, for us living here in the 21st century, a million miles away in terms of virtually every situation of our lives, how does this experience translate? Well put in simple terms I believe that it is still possible to walk in that level of fellowship with a Holy God; I have experienced times of communion and discourse that well near lifted me to heaven (metaphorically speaking) I have had revelation about situations that were otherwise unexplainable and seen visions that I had to further pray to be interpreted. We live in a time where (unlike Moses) we are filled with the Holy Spirit and have Him as Counsellor and Guide for our day to day lives. These times of increased closeness are special and are to be sought after but not (I believe) at the expense of our joy and peace in moment by moment living.

Moses did get his request granted in full; he was buried by the hand of God and appeared with the mighty Elijah in front of the terrified disciples as they witnessed the transfiguration of Christ on the mountain.

He was simply another flawed man who was privileged to serve in spite of himself, which is no more or less than any of us could hope for.

5

"Not all those who wander are lost."

J R R Tolkien

1 Corinthians 10

"I don't want you to forget, dear brothers and sisters, about our ancestors in the wilderness long ago. All of them were guided by a cloud that moved ahead of them, and all of them walked through the sea on dry ground. In the cloud and in the sea, all of them were baptized as followers of Moses. All of them ate the same spiritual food, and all of them drank the same spiritual water. For they drank from the spiritual rock that travelled with them, and that rock was Christ."

Deuteronomy 5

"The LORD our God made a covenant with us at Mount Sinai.* The LORD did not make this covenant with our ancestors, but with all of us who are alive today. At the mountain the LORD spoke to you face to face from the heart of the fire. I stood as an intermediary between you and the LORD, for you were afraid of the fire and did not want to approach the mountain. He spoke to me, and I passed his words on to you."

Moses is speaking to the nation of Israel as they stand for the second time on the banks of the

Jordan River. Forty years have come and gone and with them, the entire generation of people who had rejected the call of God. Standing before him now are all of those who were under eighteen at the time when the spies came back with their report from the land of promise; everyone else (with the exception of Caleb and Joshua) have fallen in the wilderness, victims of their own disobedience.

The new leaders of this vast company of people were just children when they experienced what Moses now spoke of, it must have been one of the youngest nations ever to be formed, just two men over sixty would cross the Jordan River to establish and fulfil the ancient promise made to Abraham so many years before. During their time of wandering the people had experienced the presence of a Holy God on a daily basis, every time they looked over to the tabernacle they could see His presence was still with them in a very tangible way. Every morning they would collect the manna and prepare food for the day, walking on shoes that never wore out; the daily miracles were as commonplace to them as the privileges that we now enjoy are to us today. For us in the developed world, water is on tap and food is in our shops, electricity charges our gadgets and we can choose whether or not we go to church or read our bibles. Such choices are not even available to whole people groups in our world and yet we take these things as our right and treat them as things to enjoy or not.

The average person in the wilderness could make very similar choices when it came to their spiritual walk that we can; do I want to offer today's sacrifice of gratitude? Do I want to discuss the law with my kids and order my life by it? Do I want to draw nearer to God and enjoy as much fellowship with Him as I can? The level of spiritual supervision that was upon them was obviously far more onerous than most of us would now allow, but the freedom which has been given to us under grace allows us to choose to draw nearer in a much freer sense.

The purpose of this chapter is to explore what privileges these people enjoyed in spite of putting themselves into a place of judgement and then to look at how the next generation grew up within that framework until it was their time to move forward in God's purposes; and hopefully to gather a few lessons for ourselves along the way.

Having made their position clear to Moses when the audible voice boomed from the mountain with fire and smoke, they turned to Joshua to make them an Idol; even while Moses was still on the mountain receiving the commands of God for them, they were melting their gold in the fire. When that episode was over they experienced several other devastating displays of God's holiness and judgement where He established exactly how this relationship which they had chosen was going to operate in practice. As is always the case in a new way of living within a relationship, boundaries need to be set and frictions overcome as each party finds a way of working. In the early days of our marriage my wife and I exchanged many misunderstandings for resolutions as we slowly came to understand how each other operated on a day to day basis. God in His mercy meets with them through the priesthood and directly through Moses; life settles down and the people get to work manufacturing the tabernacle and its attendant furniture, also the utensils required to function as a worshipful people. Intrinsically linked to the tabernacle was their method of government; this was a Theocratic ruler- ship with God as the King and Moses with the priests and elders as His ministers.

There is no doubt that the people were fully involved when it came to the making of their place of worship; whether it was by the contribution of their wealth (plundered from Egypt as they left) or the time and skills, it took a considerable amount of effort to build this exactly as described to Moses on the mountain. The importance of getting it correct cannot be overstated; Moses was clearly told:

"Be sure that you make everything according to the pattern I have shown you here on the mountain." Exodus 25:40

Because

"That is why the Tabernacle and everything in it, which were copies of things in heaven, had to be purified by the blood of animals. But the real things in heaven had to be purified with far better sacrifices than the blood of animals."

Hebrews 9:23

As such was not open to interpretation. For us living in the church age we have been given very specific information and instructions about what is important when it comes to our services i.e. the remembrance table and church structure. Moses was told

"Give these instructions to the people of Israel: The offerings you present as special gifts are a pleasing aroma to me; they are my food. See to it that they are brought at the appointed times and offered according to my instructions."

Numbers 28:2

In some way which is beyond our understanding God takes delight in the willing offering of a little human in obedience to His commands. Likewise as His people gather to remember the death of His son there is a delight that comes to His heart and as the Angels observe the Godly order within the church they look on in wonder (1 Corinthians 11). It would be an understatement to say that two millennia of distance have made the church something of a mess; however, when a group of Christians draw aside to glorify Christ, the heavens take notice.

Now clearly the children of Israel weren't sitting around all day for forty years just breaking commands and offering sacrifices. In a camp of that size there were a huge amount of things to be done and organised. Aside from the religious aspects, there were families to raise, teach and feed; there were soldiers to equip with weapons and armour and training to be arranged. The thousands of animals that were required for the offerings had to be reared, fed and cared for; in short, this mobile city was a hive of activity and a model of efficiency that it could be packed up and moved at short notice whenever the cloud moved. That there is only a few recorded mumblings and insurrections over those years is something for wonderment more than head shaking.

Psalm 77:20 records that

"You led your people along that road like a flock of sheep, with Moses and Aaron as their shepherds."

The picture that is presented here is one of great gentleness and care, as each area became stripped of vegetation and the surrounding human waste became insanitary the great Shepherd moved them on to a new place. What strikes me in the renewed study of this great nation is that the Lord loved them in spite of themselves; even although they had rejected the closeness that He wanted them all to enjoy He still worked within the parameters that they would allow. Ever loving and hopeful, He cares and draws and loves from the middle of their camp from within the tabernacle. This is not to suggest that He was waiting like some lovesick puppy begging for attention; He is and was a Holy God who demanded a standard of holiness from His people that saw law breakers and diseased people put outside the camp until they were clean again and fit to return to the protection and care of camp. We must never imagine that God is sitting waiting for my call and will jump when I have decided to be ready; the Hebrew writer pleads with us to be very careful that we do not miss out on the spiritual blessings that are ours by inheritance as children of the new covenant.

"God's promise of entering his rest still stands, so we ought to tremble with fear that some of you might fail to experience it. For this good news—that God has prepared this rest—has been announced to us just as it was to them. But it did them no good because they didn't share the faith of those who listened to God. For only we who believe can enter his rest"

Hebrews 4:1-3

Yes He is our Father and as such will receive a repentant son back home, but the warnings of Paul to the Corinthians about getting things in order within the church cannot be overlooked (Chapter 11). Equally the warnings of discipline are as relevant today as ever they were.

It is clear that in Deuteronomy Moses is reiterating to a new generation all that has gone before; a large percentage of those over forty would have been at the foot of Sinai and would have walked through the sea to get there, but everyone else had only heard about these things. It was to be a feature of the nation of Israel that they reminded themselves often of their humble beginnings, many passages of Scripture run through the history of this nation by way of encouraging the hearts of a new generation to service. It is interesting that Paul in the passage quoted at the start of this chapter connects the spiritual growth and instruction that they received in the wilderness to Christ. Every animal that died in offering or sacrifice pointed to Him, every dove, pigeon or grain offered on the altar spoke of Him; the priest and the ark pointed to Him and although they never knew it at the time they were fulfilling picture after picture of Christ.

So when Moses disobeyed the instruction to speak to the rock and struck it instead, he weakened the authority and holiness of God in the eyes of the people (Numbers 20). God was not weakened or lessened in any way, but in the eyes of all watching, even the slightest perception of that was unacceptable to God. Those who take the position of leadership have a tremendous responsibility placed upon them to represent the Glory and holiness of God.

This new generation were completely and utterly reckoned as being under the same covenant as their parents, Moses says it is because they stood at the mountain, Paul adds that it was also a spiritual aspect that united them together in Christ. The amazing point about it all is that for a people who lived and died because of their rejection and disobedience, and for a completely new generation who were born into a situation not of their own making there was this wonderful spiritual relationship with God. The fact that all of the people who succeeded those who died had such a connection with God and a deep understanding of their heritage and place before God proves that the majority of the nation did actually live it correctly and followed the teaching they had received.

In the forty plus years that I have myself wandered this earth I have attended and been a member of many churches of varying shades, I have encountered and befriended hundreds of people and walked closely with a mixture of people with a diversity of passions and backgrounds. In all of that time I have spent with Christians I would say that with very few exceptions they loved the Lord and wanted to walk in a way that pleased Him; that love found its expression in many different ways but still their desire was to do right.

It would be fair to say that there are those who seek position at the expense of love and mercy but they are mercifully very few; there are those who have stumbled and others who have found themselves jaded by life, still others (like myself) have just been worn out and lost their way a bit. The opportunity to start over is one of the greatest things about our faith in Christ; I started out by sharing my need to return to a simplicity and a renewed appreciation of God in Christ Jesus, and to this point He has been drawing my heart slowly back to His as I have studied these pages of Scripture and His chosen people. He is once again opening the door to His heart and opening mine by degrees to an appreciation of Himself.

As this great people took their place and gathered at the Jordan river once more, they listened to the final address of a man who desperately wanted to please God, who had become His friend in spite of his own fears and failures and went closer into the heart of God than most ever do; who had been taught in many circumstances over many years to obey and lead in humility, and who's heart was broken at the thought of not finishing the job. It should have been so simple, lead them out - lead them in; but people are not simple, they are complicated and stubborn, they have their own minds and a free will which God has given to them. But Moses loved this multitude of people and was willing to pass them on to the care of Joshua, his great concern was who would replace him; and having settled this matter in his own mind, he could die in peace. For them, the excitement was fresh, the challenge was waiting and it was theirs for the taking.

6

**"The Lord your God will drive those nations
out ahead of you little by little. You will not
clear them away all at once, otherwise the
wild animals would multiply too quickly for
you.** Deuteronomy 7:22"

For many years the crossing of Jordan has
signified the moving from this life to the next as
we finally enter into the land of rest and
promise. There have been countless songs

written with this as the central theme; these songs primarily (but not exclusively, since the British nationalistic and Empirical attitude also pervaded the church) came out of the USA and were from the second half of the eighteenth century and on into the first half of the twentieth century; during that time popular church culture grabbed hold of the idea that had been key to the survival of negro slaves who were living tortuous lives, that this world was our wilderness and the promised land was heaven.

Coupled to that is the American idea of being 'one nation under God' and having the Mosaic covenant psyche deeply ingrained into them as a nation. This (in part) explains the idea of having a divine mandate to protect the world and the constant thought of God being intrinsically involved in every storm, blessing and sports event. Having a God conscious centrality in all things isn't a bad thing because He truly does know every minute detail of His creation, but we are not Israelites under a Mosaic covenant today, neither have we replaced the true sons of Abraham in God's eternal purposes, in spite of the popular teaching of the replacement theologians (although they have been set aside for a time as Paul states in Romans 10) we are children of a new covenant, a new and living way under Christ. The blessing we now enjoy is primarily a spiritual one and not earth bound; the slaves of the American south understood this only too well, as they saw their white plantation owners grow rich on the backs of destitute cotton pickers while quoting Scripture to justify the harsh treatment of their workers. John Newton the great hymn writer and preacher also had to confront his own attitude towards the slaves he was transporting from Africa to America in the light of the words of Scripture. Many have assumed that he shunned his position as slave transporter after his conversion but his realisation of the barbarity of the trade took some years to percolate in him.

When Moses had died and Joshua took the reins, he sought the mind of God as to how to move things forward, and the battle begins in earnest for their inheritance. The key flaw to the whole spiritualising of Jordan is, that for us, there is no battle to be fought when we cross over (Paul describes the final moment on earth as glorious victory in 1 Corinthians 15) all of our battles are now and the promised rest is, for us, while still here on earth on the journey to heaven; with the ultimate fulfilment being at the end of life when we pass from the darkness of this world and move on into the fullness of our redemption and freedom from sin.

So having spent their lives moving from place to place and functioning as a nation in one central community; they were trained, ready and willing to have a place of their own to settle in. They had conquered the people on the Eastern side of the Jordan River and were massing there in preparation for the assault on Canaan. As the two spies leave to scout out the land Joshua readies himself to lead and the people are instructed to purify themselves in preparation to cross the river. The tribes of Rueben, Gad and the half tribe of Manasseh had already received their allotment of land with the condition that they must assist in the capture of everything on the other side. When you consider the scale of the area which God had promised to them, it is incredibly vast; reaching East to the Euphrates river, from Egypt in the South to Lebanon in the North and bordered on the west by the mighty Mediterranean Sea. Only under king David did they ever rule this whole area, only for Solomon to gradually squander it over his lifetime.

Our interest in this stage of Israel's history isn't purely historical; the principles contained throughout Scripture are repeated over and again in God's dealings with mankind. Whether He is taking an entire nation of people to

Himself or calling an individual into service, the principles stay true to His unchanging character and are always based upon love, sacrifice and fellowship, and generally in that order.

The calling from Egypt is better equated to the individual salvation of a soul, as we see God's heart moved to act in sending a deliverer with a message of freedom from bondage into a new and personal relationship with Himself.

The preparation of God in bringing a family of shepherds into Egypt four hundred years earlier meant that when hundreds of thousands of lambs were required for the first great Passover, they were already there. The blood of the lamb on the doorposts protected the occupants from the angel of death, and in the morning the whole nation walked out free from the life of bondage and slavery (at least physically). The meeting at the mountain introduced them to the God who had called them and to the fullness of what He had in His heart for them to enjoy. The rejection of Him

left them in a greatly reduced walk;
nevertheless they still enjoyed His presence in a
measure, albeit nothing close to His desire for
them, even when Moses was called up the
mountain with Joshua and the elders to enjoy a
covenant meal with God in Exodus 22. It says
there that it was seventy **'of'** the elders; among
the leaders of this nation some did and others
didn't go up to be with God. We could argue
that seventy was symbolic in its entirety but the
call went out to all.

As Christians our journey is very similar, we are
called from whatever circumstances that He
initially finds us in and shows us the way of
salvation in whatever particular way the Holy
Spirit applies it to our need; it always involves
the application of the cross of Christ and our sin
being dealt with there; provision having been
made there for all who will come. In order for
the new life to begin we need that initial filling
of the Holy Spirit who seals us as His own

(Ephesians 1) and so begins the unfolding of our relationship together as He reveals Himself to me and shows me the depths of my own heart. The experience of every individual is vastly different and yet basically the same, the nuances of character and life make for a study in themselves as our Creator does what He does best to fit the lessons to the uniqueness of each person.

No person is encouraged to blindly go off following Christ, He Himself warned against such action and told several parables to illustrate His point in Luke chapter 14:25-33

A large crowd was following Jesus. He turned around and said to them, "If you want to be my disciple, you must hate everyone else by comparison—your father and mother, wife and children, brothers and sisters—yes, even your own life. Otherwise, you cannot be my disciple. And if you do not carry your own

cross and follow me, you cannot be my disciple.

"But don't begin until you count the cost. For who would begin construction of a building without first calculating the cost to see if there is enough money to finish it? Otherwise, you might complete only the foundation before running out of money, and then everyone would laugh at you. They would say, 'There's the person who started that building and couldn't afford to finish it!'

"Or what king would go to war against another king without first sitting down with his counsellors to discuss whether his army of 10,000 could defeat the 20,000 soldiers marching against him? And if he can't, he will send a delegation to discuss terms of peace while the enemy is still far away. So you cannot become my disciple without giving up everything you own.

When Joshua was preparing to cross the Jordan River he didn't dig out his notes from the last time and study them; forty years had passed and this was a new time and needed new and up to date information. So he sends out the two spies to get a clearer picture of what was waiting for them; they already knew the overall picture of how good it was in there, this was battle-specific information which he was now requiring, how many, how large what defences. He knew from what had been said to him that it would be a slow process because the land was large and they would need to gradually populate it in order to govern it in even a basic way.

As Christians we imagine that we will get a Matrix type download of all the relevant information we require to live this life; in my experience that almost never happens. We get what we need at any given point of time (assuming that we are open to it) and we are taught bit by bit line upon line, experience upon experience until we are ready to go forward.

When I was learning the trumpet for the first time my teacher friend gave me some information that helped me to understand the process. He said that my progress would be uphill for a while and then I would plateau; I would not really improve greatly for another while (indeterminate) and then I would push up another hill and so on. This proved to be a very accurate description of what happened. Please don't take from this analogy that I agree with the concept of levels within Christianity, this has been used in certain circles to engender spiritual superiority and only tends towards making others feel inferior which is something that is nowhere found within Scripture.

I have found that God doesn't exhaust us completely in the general learning phase of our lives, the training can become intensive and all-consuming at times but the real exhaustion comes in the serving phase of our life. I asked

God to 'use' me as many Christians do, but we need to be aware that He will take us at our word (as mentioned earlier). After eight years of constant 'use' I was empty. I was like a wrung out cloth. People have said that God wouldn't do that to you, I say to them to read their Bible; let's throw some names around:

Noah

Abraham

Moses

David

Elijah

Jonah

Peter

Paul

Demas (he had just had enough)

And so we could continue through history, each of these men taken to that absolute limit of physical and mental exhaustion and yet totally and completely in the will of God for most of their lives. I also hear the verses being quoted that His grace is sufficient and He will not test us beyond that which we are able to bear; both true and I experienced the truth of them at the time but it doesn't change the fact that I couldn't go another step. I actually got to the point where I couldn't even string a sentence together or work out the most basic of problems. I have experienced supernatural strength during times of extended exertion and empowerment to keep going way beyond anything that I could contemplate just now, but I trust Him enough to know that my body can only take so much and needs times of rest.

He doesn't teach us so that we are taught, and shelved, we are prepared and made ready to be of use in His Kingdom.

Thank God that He does go slowly when we are being taught; otherwise we would not be able to handle all of the challenges that He sends our way when it is time for action.

7

The battle for peace.

In 1873 the Colt Peacemaker was adopted as the official sidearm for the US army; it was to have a twenty year career and became hugely iconic and popular both in the military and public sector. They were further popularised in the multitude of cowboy films churned out during the twentieth century; the problem (of course) is that no weapon can bring peace. Weapons remove threats or destroy enemies but as a means of making peace they are singularly inadequate.

If we defined peace as the absence of war we would struggle to find a decade in the history of mankind that there was any peace. As a race we have fought at family, tribal, national and international levels for the whole of our history; from Cain and Abel to the world conflagration of the 1940's. Every conflict before and since then has been about power, money and authority. Whatever other title or name is attached to it, they boil down to one or all of these things, no matter how many may claim a religious title for their struggle few religions condone bloodshed and Christ certainly never did.

When we turn to the Bible, peace has a whole different definition; particularly in the Old Testament passages that we have been looking at it was intrinsically linked to the settling of a nation and the maintaining of that nation as an earthly state. But as we have discussed previously, the primary peace was with God Himself and the outworking of that was in the governance of the nation of Israel; under the conditions of the covenant (which they had agreed through Moses and reiterated under Solomon) their national peace and prosperity was in direct correlation to their obedience to the commands of God in the Law. On a personal level, provision was firmly in place for the individual to have peace with God; not in the sense which we now enjoy, but nevertheless the peace offering was enshrined in the Law to make it possible for a person (who so desired) to have the conscious knowledge of sins forgiven and peace restored to their hearts.

Now, many religions will pursue a peaceful state of being and do offer a whole raft of ideas and ways of achieving this inner peace. Many of the practices of the Eastern religions will, and do actually allow you to achieve this state of peace with yourself and your surroundings; what they cannot offer is the knowledge of peace with God. The conscious assurance that sin is forever dealt with, that the judgement of God is no longer a threat or a fear, and that He is satisfied with me because of the cross of Christ. This fact alone makes Christianity unique among the voices crying out for our attention.

So this Biblical peace is very different from any other in that it relates to our relationship with a Holy God, the definition is:

A state of quiet or tranquillity; freedom from disturbance or agitation; calm; repose.

As we have discussed already this is achievable on a personal level from other methods, but when it is in relation to sin or any of its manifestations in our lives which break that fellowship with God, only the blood of Jesus Christ can cleanse us from the sin and its effects.

I should say at this point that 'peace' is no sure
indicator that a course of action is sanctioned
by God. I have had many conversations with
people over the years who have assured me
that they have complete peace about the
course of action that they about to take; only to
discover upon deeper digging that it is wholly
unscriptural. Of all the guidance factors to rule
out of any decision, scripture is not one of
them.

Returning to the banks of Jordan in the book of
Joshua chapter3 where we left the Israelites;
we find them prepared and ready to finally
cross over into their new home. Can you
imagine the excitement levels in the camp as
they can see this land of promise just over the
river? Years of training and wandering,
worshipping and travelling in this mobile nation
have finally culminated in a sudden moment of
realisation that, 'we just need to cross that
river, and tomorrow we do.'

Now reports vary about the width of the river during harvest (which is generally accepted to be the early harvest when the winter snows are in full melt around April) but the consensus settles around 120 yards wide and too deep to stand in even if the current would allow you to. So it represented a formidable barrier to entering into all that has been promised; no amount of weapons training can overcome a raging torrent in the days before the Bailey bridge with close to two million people. How many times we have been tantalisingly close to all that has been promised to us, we have prayed for and received a vision for our lives only to get to the point of fulfilment and see it vanish like ice on a sunny day. There are never satisfactory answers as to why some people seem to receive all that has been implanted in their hearts (never without struggle and sacrifice but nevertheless things look largely similar to the vision they earnestly sought) and many others just don't. It is very true that

God's ways are past finding out and that He has absolutely no obligation to explain Himself in any way, but I want to ask questions that many are afraid to voice in church for fear of seeming unruly. Why is it that few successful leaders ever speak of the disappointments and the unanswered questions and prayers, the nights of uncertainty about their calling and deep rumblings that nobody ever hears. I appreciate that these are not saleable and would 'seem' to reflect badly on a God of hope and certainty but in actuality the reverse is true. The Holy Spirit never hid the faults and doubts, questions and fears of His servants; we have looked at some already but Moses, Abraham and Elijah to name but a few were not quiet about their issues. Read the Psalms and listen to David venting his spleen about the injustice and unfairness of life while God (seemingly) remains silent and distant.

You are not alone having such thoughts; I have spent many nights and days ruminating over such things and freely acknowledge that many things will not be answered. I have come to trust in the unseen hand of an Almighty God who has my best interests always at heart. Having committed my life to Him I allow Him the freedom to work in and through me without hindrance (mostly) for the purposes of eternal value. That's not to say that I don't get ticked off and annoyed at times when frustration creeps in, but I have made a covenant with God and He with me which is eternal in its scope and I do not have all of the answers.

Many times I remind myself of this as my children want to know the infinitesimal details of everything that we have arranged and I hear myself say things like "will you allow me to be the parent?" Sometimes it seems that I hear God whisper the same to me, "will you let me be God?"

Without going too deeply into the verses that follow, what happened next was incredible. The priests carried the ark of God to the river bank and as their feet touched the water it stopped flowing and was held back on the right hand side of them and banked up like a wall. Again this multitude of people crossed over on 'dry' ground; it is a small but significant point that it was dry ground. Not for them a slopping around in mud in their forty year old shoes; I have no difficulty with such passages and feel no requirement to explain them naturally. If we fall into the trap of trying to rationalise and understand the intricacies of these events we are in danger of reducing them to the mundanity of everyday events. These were supernatural events with a definitive purpose as we shall see in a moment; I fully believe that if we are open to God working the miraculous we may be privileged at times to experience it first-hand. So many things in my life cannot be simply explained away without an understanding of a supernatural God at work.

The day had finally arrived; the priests had lifted the Ark up on to their shoulders and set off. When they are half a mile out everyone sets off behind them keeping that set distance between them until the way is clear to follow on. It is recorded in Joshua 4:16:

"As soon as the feet of the priests who were carrying the Ark touched the water at the river's edge, the water above the point began backing up a great distance away."

At that point, the rest of the people moved forward and by the time that they had travelled the half mile the crossing was ready.

Now, if you feel like it you can go Google this event and give yourself a headache with the thousands of explanations, arguments over crossing points, how far away the town was the river backed up to and two million other dissected nuances of a two verse record. Or, you can decide that a God who created a universe in 6 days and gave us a scant description at the start of Genesis of how He did it; says that a river (which He created from rain that He put in place by evaporation from an ocean which He put there, runs down a mountain side to begin the process over again) flowed backwards on itself, piling up as it went and stopped flowing. If that is the God whom you worship? Then just maybe the Bible became whole lot simpler to understand! We have become too clever by far, and we imagine that we can outthink this ancient God who could fool a simpler people from a simpler time. Look what *we* can do now God, Paul wrote to the Corinthians and told them that:

"The foolish plan of God is wiser than the wisest of human plans."

So these priests stood there in the middle of the river until every man, woman, child and animal had settled on the other side. They stood until 12 large stones had been removed to the bank and set up as a reminder; and when 12 more stones were set up on the river bed they were finally allowed to walk up out of the Jordan. As soon as these men had settled on the bank the river returned to its former state.

I had said that it was important that this event was seen by all around and the rumour of it spread quickly up the Mediterranean coastline on the other side of the country. The term used by Joshua is that they were

"Paralyzed by fear."

This was why God made it such a dramatic crossing, because the following day there was to be a renewing of the covenant by circumcision. Absolutely nothing that is recorded is for no reason; these details are very important to notice because they are each significant in their own way.

So where do we fit into this entire picture?

I have already said that I believe the Jordan equals death connection to be flawed; so how do we equate this to ourselves? I believe that the salvation experience is clearly pictured for us in these verses.

- The Ark going ahead to prepare the way that we pass from our old place of being to our place of inheritance – the Ark of the Covenant was always a picture of Christ and Him being the Mercy seat where God and man met together.
- The river going backwards to allow safe dry passage – Christ has opened the way for all who would cross from death to life, there is no great effort required, just a simple believing step of faith.
- The Ark remaining in the river bed so each person had to pass by it –there is no way to God but by Christ.
- The priests remaining still until the last person were over – The door remains open until every child is called in.
- The permanent reminder set up beside the place of crossing over – The

communion table is a permanent reminder of the cross and what was accomplished there.

- The renewing of circumcision as a sign of the covenant – We are all baptised as a public sign of the covenant which we have made with God.

There are many other applications of the events but these are how they appealed to me in connection with this chapter.

Having the entire male population lying in agony for a week would have left the camp in a very vulnerable position; so we see why there was such a need to have this *'fear'* come over the inhabitants of the land which they had now entered. I should say that I don't equate baptism with circumcision, it was a totally different time for them and Paul states clearly in Romans 2 that our circumcision is in our hearts; and furthermore that our sin and shame was completely dealt with at the cross.

What follows in the book of Joshua is the reason for the title of this chapter; we are not going to go through each battle individually but they serve to remind us that after salvation comes the real battle. God could have sent the flood waters across the nation and swept it clean for them, or brought a foreign army in to annihilate the inhabitants; however, this was to be their own personal battle for their own plot of land.

It comes back around to the same central theme which we have been discussing; you want it? You go get it. What do you lack? Ask and you shall receive it.

"Search for peace and work to maintain it." 1Peter 3:11

Peter made no bones about it; did he not understand what Jesus said in John 14:27?

"I am leaving you with a gift – peace of mind and heart. And the peace I give is a gift the world cannot give."

Of course he did, but he also knew how fragile that peace was in those early days of the church. He himself shattered that peace many times over his lifetime; and now writing as an old man, he encourages others to follow what he has learned by hard experience.

Paul's final words to the Corinthian believers were:

"Be joyful, Grow to maturity. Encourage each other. Live in harmony and peace. Then the God of love and peace will be with you."

To the Ephesians in Chapter4:

"Make every effort to keep yourselves united in the Spirit, binding yourselves together with peace."

To the Colossians in Chapter 3:

"And let the peace that comes from Christ rule in your hearts."

To the Thessalonians in the second letter 3:16

"Now may the Lord of peace Himself give you His peace at all times and in every situation."

I would love to say that I fully live in this state; I have had times in my live where it has been my experience to enjoy extended periods of rest and peace in Christ; and other times where it was anything but peace. That was the inspiration for writing this chapter; I believe many Christian labour under the false impression that there are these super – saints who float around 'Angel – like' in an exalted plain untroubled by the common ills that beset us lesser beings. I tend to think that they are not operating a full disclosure policy.

The final point about this event before we leave it is simply this. It has been my experience in watching many people come to new birth over the years, that there seems to be this period where the new Christian is placed within a bubble. Let me explain what I mean by that.

When I first fell in love with my wife (and this is not unique) I was in a giddy exalted state. I was quite unaware that a change had taken place in my walk; my demeanour, my attitude and generally my whole disposition was different. A friend at work who was 18 years down the line from me took me aside one day and said this, "you don't realise how special this time is that you are in now, please fully enjoy it because at some point in next year it is going to gradually slip away and never return."

And he was correct. It did just gradually lessen and settle into a more stable and calm place. I love my wife in ways now that I couldn't have imagined during that giddy phase but the love is not less.

Here's the point if you haven't already got it.

Most new Christians experience a very similar 'jolt' of power from the Holy Spirit as He comes to seal and indwell them; it manifests in as many different ways as there are people who receive Him (we legislate this at our peril, it is not a prescribed thing). Some people receive instant deliverance from addictions or behaviours, some are healed of illnesses; others run around telling everyone they meet about this new life they have found, still others just want to retreat in to a room and quietly worship for six months.

LET THEM!

We want to get them 'hooked up' with a programme, or whatever and get them through whatever our church method is for new believers. Here's a novel idea; what if we asked God what this particular individual needs to let them grow into this life that have begun. Well that takes commitment, time, energy and specific attention which many churches simply can't be bothered to commit to. When the

Israelite men were lying groaning, God made sure that they were left alone; sometimes that is what I pray the sincere well-wishers seeking to push the new converts into the prescribed programmes would do. We are so uniquely created by a creative God, but we reduce everything to its simplest format and often quash that early joy which new believers are experiencing.

My work friend was so gentle, he wasn't laughing at my giddy state; he was reminded of a time when he too skipped around his new love and wanted a young man to fully appreciate what he had.

8

In the nine months that I have been writing this, a lot has changed. Slowly and gently I have been experiencing the things that I have been writing about; as I have re-opened the door to my heart He has been opening my spiritual eyes to things that I have long known, but put in a drawer last year.

By no means am I even close to many of the things that I have written down on some of these pages, but the journey has begun and with it the hope of again experiencing what I have previously lived.

I understand the heart that cries out for a restoration of that 'first love;' I too would love that again, but is that what the Lord asked them to do in Revelation 2? Look what He actually said:

"Nevertheless I have somewhat against thee, because thou hast left thy first love. Remember therefore from whence thou art fallen, and repent, and do the first <u>works</u>;" (KJV)

As my friend at work correctly pointed out with regards to earthly love, "you don't get this again." So in church, why are pursuing something that was a new birth experience? The New Testament writers were pretty basic when they told the believers to 'man up' and go to maturity! The risen Lord never asked them to return to that first love feeling, He told them to get back and to do what you already know. This biblical love is not romantic gushy Hollywood love; it is the reasoned out love of Romans chapter 2, in view of what He has done for you then you must logically do as He has instructed.

Now I appreciate that this sounds very hard and cold hearted and it is only one side of the coin; but, if we sit around waiting to 'feel' the love we may sit around waiting for a long time. With maturity comes the expectation that we will just do certain things that we know are correct; harrumphing around bemoaning what is missing while neglecting what isn't is never going to be an excuse at the Judgement seat.

I need to toughen up; the church needs to toughen up and stop expecting to be spoon fed when we know already what to do. Micah in the Old Testament addressed a very similar situation in the nation of Israel in his day; people were asking what they should do to atone for their sins (Chapter6:7-8) and his answer was very succinct:

"The Lord has told you what is good, and this is what He requires of you: to do what is right, to

love mercy, and to walk humbly with your God."

Right there I have a prescription for my spiritual malaise; if I don't know what to do next? Do that; and work forward from there. I too, long for the closeness and fellowship of the Lord, but I also waste hours not making time for that to happen. This morning I was listening to Jerry Lee Lewis singing, "In the Garden" and it reminded me that for near on 4 years I would rise early at least a couple of times a week to do what he was singing about

I come to the garden alone
While the dew is still on the roses
And the voice I hear falling on my ear
The Son of God discloses.

Refrain

And He walks with me, and He talks with me,
And He tells me I am His own;

And the joy we share as we tarry there,
None other has ever known.

Words: Charles Austin Miles (1912)

I (like most people) am my own worst enemy,
and always will be; but by the grace and mercy
of God I am going to do this again, and if I can,
so can you.

Printed in Great Britain
by Amazon

17713262R00079